Thinking Critically

Thinking Critically:
Cell Phones

Bradley Steffens

ReferencePoint
Press®

San Diego, CA

© 2018 ReferencePoint Press, Inc.
Printed in the United States

For more information, contact:
ReferencePoint Press, Inc.
PO Box 27779
San Diego, CA 92198
www.ReferencePointPress.com

Picture Credits:
All charts and graphs by Maury Aaseng

LIBRARY OF CONGRESS CATALOGING-IN-PUBLICATION DATA

Name: Steffens, Bradley, 1955– author.
Title: Thinking Critically: Cell Phones/by Bradley Steffens.
Description: San Diego, CA: ReferencePoint Press, Inc., [2018] | Series: Thinking Critically |
    Includes bibliographical references and index.
Identifiers: LCCN 2017040656 (print) | LCCN 2017044952 (ebook) | ISBN 9781682823361 (ebook)
    | ISBN 9781682823354 (hardback)
Subjects: LCSH: Cell phones—Social aspects—Juvenile literature. | Smartphones—Social
    aspects—Juvenile literature.
Classification: LCC HE9713 (ebook) | LCC HE9713 .S725 2018 (print) | DDC 384.5/34—dc23
LC record available at https://lccn.loc.gov/2017040656

Contents

"Literacy is the most basic currency of the knowledge economy we're living in today." Barack Obama (at the time a senator from Illinois) spoke these words during a 2005 speech before the American Library Association. One question raised by this statement is: What does it mean to be a literate person in the twenty-first century?

E.D. Hirsch Jr., author of *Cultural Literacy: What Every American Needs to Know*, answers the question this way: "To be culturally literate is to possess the basic information needed to thrive in the modern world. The breadth of the information is great, extending over the major domains of human activity from sports to science."

But literacy in the twenty-first century goes beyond the accumulation of knowledge gained through study and experience and expanded over time. Now more than ever literacy requires the ability to sift through and evaluate vast amounts of information and, as the authors of the Common Core State Standards state, to "demonstrate the cogent reasoning and use of evidence that is essential to both private deliberation and responsible citizenship in a democratic republic."

The *Thinking Critically* series challenges students to become discerning readers, to think independently, and to engage and develop their skills as critical thinkers. Through a narrative-driven, pro/con format, the series introduces students to the complex issues that dominate public discourse—topics such as gun control and violence, social networking, and medical marijuana. Each chapter revolves around a single, pointed question such as Can Stronger Gun Control Measures Prevent Mass Shootings?, or Does Social Networking Benefit Society?, or Should Medical Marijuana Be Legalized? This inquiry-based approach introduces student researchers to core issues and concerns on a given topic. Each chapter includes one part that argues the affirmative and one part that argues the negative—all written by a single author. With the single-author format the predominant arguments for and against an issue can be synthesized into clear, accessible discussions supported by details and evidence including relevant facts, direct quotes, current examples, and statistical illustrations. All volumes include focus questions to guide students as they read each pro/con discussion, a list of key facts, and an annotated list of related organizations and websites for conducting further research.

The authors of the Common Core State Standards have set out the particular qualities that a literate person in the twenty-first century must have. These include the ability to think independently, establish a base of knowledge across a wide range of subjects, engage in open-minded but discerning reading and listening, know how to use and evaluate evidence, and appreciate and understand diverse perspectives. The new *Thinking Critically* series supports these goals by providing a solid introduction to the study of pro/con issues.

Cell Phones Are Changing the World

The art exhibit at the 14th Factory gallery in Los Angeles cried out to be the backdrop for a selfie. It consisted of dozens of modern sculptures depicting crowns, each displayed atop a small pedestal. A young woman crouched down by one of the pedestals to take a selfie from an angle that would make it appear as if one of the crowns were on her head. Before she could snap the picture, however, she lost her balance and fell backwards, into the pedestal. Not anchored to the floor, the freestanding pedestal toppled into the one beside it, which in turn knocked over the next one, and so on, like a row of falling dominoes. The gallery's video surveillance system recorded it all. When a video of the mishap was posted online in July 2017, it went viral. Some people who saw the pedestals falling in such an orderly fashion thought the scene was staged. It was not. The woman's careless picture taking caused $200,000 worth of damage to the fragile artworks.

The 14th Factory disaster was not the first time a cell phone–wielding tourist destroyed a priceless work of art. In 2016 a visitor to Lisbon's National Museum of Ancient Art knocked over a rare eighteenth-century statue while trying to take a selfie. The statue broke into several pieces when it hit the floor, causing irreversible damage, according to museum officials. Several museums, including the Van Gogh Museum in Amsterdam, have banned selfies to prevent such mishaps and encourage people to engage more directly with the art on display.

Cell phone users focused on their devices can become oblivious to their surroundings, posing a danger to themselves. In 2017 a tourist was bitten by a crocodile while trying to take a selfie in Thailand, and another woman fell 60 feet (18 m) from the Foresthill Bridge in California while trying to take a photo of herself. "They were taking a picture on the bridge, and then the big bolts that are holding the beams together, she stepped on them kind of weirdly and lost balance and fell backwards,"[1] her friend told a reporter from CBS Sacramento. Fortunately, both women—the one in Thailand and the woman in California—survived. A visitor to Croatia's Plitvice Lakes National Park was not so fortunate, falling to his death after venturing off an approved trail to take a selfie.

The Lure of Connection

A study by the National Safety Council has shown that 26 percent of automobile crashes in the United States are the result of drivers being distracted by their mobile devices. All states except for Arizona, Montana, Missouri, and Texas have passed laws that ban texting and other messaging while driving. Pedestrians using cell phones are also putting themselves in harm's way. The Governors Highway Safety Association reported that pedestrian deaths increased 11 percent nationwide from 2015 to 2016 due to careless cell phone use. In 2017 Honolulu, Hawaii, became the first city in the United States to make it illegal for pedestrians to cross a street or highway while viewing a mobile electronic device. "Sometimes I wish there were laws we did not have to pass, that perhaps common sense would prevail," said Honolulu mayor Kirk Caldwell. "But sometimes we lack common sense."[2]

Drivers and pedestrians can be distracted by talking to another person, sipping a beverage, or reading a note, but cell phones are especially engrossing since they are packed with interactive capabilities and rich media, including music, videos, pictures, and live chat. In addition, cell phones are constantly fed new content in a steady stream, or feed. The lure of what people are saying and doing in social media can be almost irresistible to the cell phone user. In 2016 the technology research firm Dscout used an embedded app to track every tap, swipe, and click by a group of cell phone users over a five-day period. The researchers found

More than 5 Billion Cell Phone Users Worldwide by 2019

The online data analytics company Statistica forecasts a steadily increasing number of cell phone (or mobile phone) users worldwide. The company estimates that number will exceed 5 billion by 2019, thanks in large part to the growing popularity of smartphones. Smartphone use, which was about 38 percent in 2014, was expected to reach more than 50 percent of mobile users by 2018. By 2019, the company expects there to be 2.7 billion smartphone users worldwide.

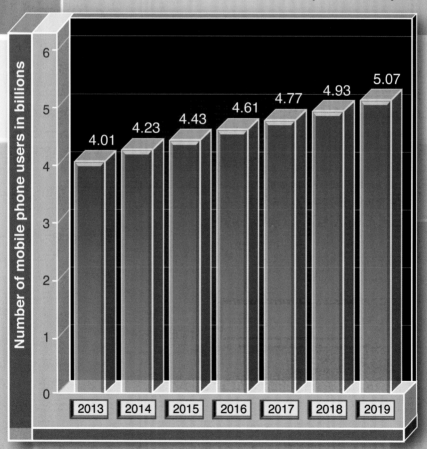

Number of mobile phone users worldwide from 2013 to 2019 (in billions)

Number of mobile phone users in billions

- 2013: 4.01
- 2014: 4.23
- 2015: 4.43
- 2016: 4.61
- 2017: 4.77
- 2018: 4.93
- 2019: 5.07

Source: Statistica.com, "Number of Mobile Phone Users Worldwide from 2013 to 2019 (in Billions)," 2017. www.statistica.com.

that users touched their cell phones an average of 2,617 times a day to check on social media updates, play or skip songs, send or read text messages, upload pictures or videos, make calls, check the time, and perform other tasks. Heavy users registered more than 5,000 touches per day. That is a lot of interaction and, often, a lot of distraction.

An Essential Part of Modern Life

Despite the potential for distraction and even danger, billions of people worldwide own cell phones and consider them an essential part of modern life. For example, a 2017 study by the Pew Research Center found that 95 percent of Americans own a cell phone. The share of Americans who own smartphones—cell phones capable of connecting to the Internet and running various applications (apps)—is now 77 percent, up from just 35 percent when Pew conducted its first survey of smartphone ownership in 2011. Smartphones reached a 40 percent market saturation in their first two and a half years on the market, matching television as the consumer technology with the fastest adoption rate.

Today, 4.9 billion people worldwide have cell phones, 2.6 billion of which are smartphones. The number of smartphones is expected to grow to 6 billion by 2020. In many countries, especially in the developing world, more people connect to the Internet with smartphones than with computers. For example, in India, the country's 204 million smartphone users are responsible for 72 percent of the nation's Internet traffic. In Nigeria, more than 80 percent of the country's web traffic is through smartphones.

With the addition of new software apps to cell phones every day and increased connection to the Internet through free wireless local networks, known as Wi-Fi, and paid data plans through cell phone service providers, people are spending increasing amounts of time using their cell phones. According to the media research firm TechCrunch, time spent on mobile apps exceeded time spent watching television for US consumers in 2015, with the average adult spending more than four hours a day on a cell phone. According to media analysts at the firm MediaKix, a third of that time is spent on social media platforms such as YouTube, Facebook, Snapchat, Instagram, and Twitter. Over a lifetime, the hours add up. MediaKix estimates that the average user will spend five years and four months on social media over a lifetime. That is more time than they will spend eating and drinking (three years and five months), grooming (one year and ten months), socializing (one year and three months), and doing laundry (six months).

Cell phones, however, are not just for fun and games. They have become the basis of big business as well. Entire industries, such as ride sharing, have grown up around cell phones and their global positioning satellite (GPS) and communications capabilities. In some US businesses, such as the publisher of *Wired*, the cell phone has replaced the personal computer as the computing device of choice. "We're at the point where anyone armed with a current model smartphone or tablet is able to handle almost all of their at-home—and even at-work—tasks without needing anything else,"[3] writes *Wired* editor Christina Bonnington.

> "Anyone armed with a current model smartphone or tablet is able to handle almost all of their at-home—and even at-work—tasks without needing anything else."[3]
>
> —Christina Bonnington, editor of *Wired* magazine

The trend is even stronger in developing countries, where traditional computers are expensive and replacement parts are in short supply. "In emerging markets, many consumers experienced the Internet, e-mail, and apps through a phone first,"[4] writes Carolina Milanesi, chief of research at Kantar Worldpanel ComTec, a global market research firm.

The Gateway to Pervasive Computing

The importance of cell phones will become even more apparent as more people use intelligent personal assistants (IPAs) such as Apple's Siri, Microsoft's Cortana, and Viv Labs' Viv, which are able to translate spoken instructions into concrete actions, using cell phone apps and communications. For example, in 2016 researchers at IPA developer Viv ordered pizzas for the entire development team simply by telling Viv what sizes and kinds of pizzas they wanted. They even changed the order several times to make the task more difficult. Viv messaged the pizza restaurant, placed the order, and paid the bill online. Forty-five minutes later the pizzas arrived at the office exactly as ordered. The Viv Labs story is an example of what is known as pervasive computing, in which machines communicate with other machines to simplify life for the computer user.

Cell phones are at the center of pervasive computing, providing the primary point of contact for people to command the vast network of interconnected machines known as the Internet of Things.

By accessing the Internet's immense amounts of interconnected software and data, cell phones are becoming an extension of the user, says Amber Case. Case is a Harvard University anthropologist who studies the relationship between humans and technology, a field known as cyborg anthropology. "It's not just a phone," she told a TEDx conference in 2015, "it's a kind of a mental exoskeleton. It's an external part of your brain."[5] This external brain boosts the capability of the inner brain, just as earlier tools, such as the hammer, ax, and knife, increased the capabilities of the human hand. "We are all cyborgs now,"[6] says Case. Tim Wu, a professor at Columbia Law School, agrees. "We are now different creatures than we once were, evolving technologically rather than biologically, in directions we must hope are for the best."[7]

> "We are all cyborgs now."[6]
>
> —Amber Case, an anthropologist at Harvard University

Chapter One

Are Cell Phones Affecting Human Relationships?

Cell Phones Bring People Together

- Cell phones enable people to communicate anytime, anywhere.
- Cell phones allow people to share pictures and videos about their lives.
- Video calls enable nonverbal communication that improves understanding.

The Debate at a Glance

Cell Phones Push People Apart

- Cell phone users retreat into their devices and ignore people around them.
- People consciously use their cell phones to avoid people and conversations.
- Cell phones give an illusion of connectedness that diminishes genuine empathy.

Cell Phones Bring People Together

"Smartphones are helping us to be more human, helping us to connect with each other."

—Amber Case, an anthropologist at Harvard University

Quoted in Yo Zushi, "Life with a Smartphone Is Like Having a Second Brain in Your Pocket," *New Statesman*, February 22, 2017. www.newstatesman.com.

Consider these questions as you read:

1. How persuasive is the argument that more frequent contact—no matter how that contact occurs—brings people together? Explain your answer.
2. Do you think video chat improves communication because it allows people to see each other's facial expressions as they talk? Why or why not?
3. Have cell phones enhanced your relationships with your parents and other family members? If so, in what ways? If not, why not?

Editor's note: The discussion that follows presents common arguments made in support of this perspective, reinforced by facts, quotes, and examples taken from various sources.

Cell phones are doing more to bring people together than any device since the advent of the telephone more than 140 years ago. Equipped with the proper hardware and software, cell phones allow people to see, speak, and write to each other—singly or in groups—at virtually any time and in any place. As a result, communication is flowing between individuals as never before. People who might have seen one another once or twice a year, or talked on the telephone on birthdays and holidays, often are in contact every day.

Anytime, Anywhere Connectivity

The original cell phones, named for the cell, or area, covered by a radio antenna that allows radio signals to flow to and from the mobile phones, were simply telephones without wires. People used them only to talk. The great advantage was that the user could be on the move rather than tethered to a telephone line when making or receiving a call. This was a revolution unto itself. People no longer had to be at home or in an office to communicate, as they did with landlines. They could be reached anytime, anywhere, indoors or out. The number of missed calls decreased because people carried their phones with them.

The ability to call for assistance from the scenes of accidents, fires, or medical emergencies saved lives. The personal safety capabilities of cell phones have transformed society. A survey conducted in 2014 by cell phone service provider Vodaphone found that 95 percent of teenagers felt safer leaving the house with their phone, mainly so they could call parents if they had a problem. Twenty percent of parents felt the same way, saying they did not permit their children to leave the house without a phone. Nevertheless, not all the early cell phone communication was a matter of life and death. Most of it was mundane: parents checking on children, friends making spur-of-the-moment plans, couples calling to say hi. People were becoming more connected.

Communicating Silently via Text Messaging

Cell phone makers soon realized that the digital display that showed the number being dialed or the number of an incoming call could also be used for displaying words sent between wireless phones. This function became known as short message service (SMS) text messaging. It allowed people to communicate during situations in which calling was not practical, such as meetings, lectures, and even meals. Brief messages such as "running late," "meeting canceled," or "flight delayed" saved cell phone users countless hours, reduced anxiety, and made people feel more connected.

Cell phones have brought people together in ways they could not have foreseen, according to Jenny Lanker, a wellness expert in Mount Vernon, Washington. Jenny's husband, Russ, served in the US Navy for

Cell Phones Have a Positive Impact on Relationships

Convergys, a market research company, surveyed one thousand adults and 201 teens on behalf of Bank of America from May 25 through June 3, 2017, to learn about their cell phone use and attitudes. The survey found that far more cell phone users believe that their devices have a positive impact on their relationships than believe they have a negative impact. Clearly, cell phones bring people together, rather than push them apart.

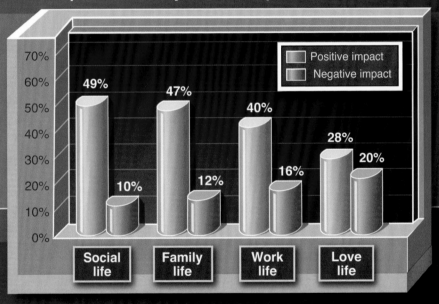

Most Americans think mobile phones have positive impact on the key relationships in their lives

Legend:
- Positive impact
- Negative impact

Social life: 49% / 10%
Family life: 47% / 12%
Work life: 40% / 16%
Love life: 28% / 20%

Source: Bank of America, "Trends in Mobility Report," August 17, 2017. http://newsroom.bankofamerica.com.

twenty-four years, which included many deployments that took him away for months at a time. After retiring, he took a job as a pilot, and Jenny expected that they would spend more time together. However, Russ's flying assignments required him to spend even more time away. "My loneliness got the best of me and I wanted to quit the marriage so many times," says Jenny. After the terrorist attacks on September 11, 2001, in which airliners were hijacked, Russ and Jenny purchased their first cell phones. The ability to reach each other via text, voice, and eventually video changed everything. "Never again was I to be kept separated from him during an emergency when there was a way to connect directly anytime I wished," says Jenny. "I wouldn't have made it through all the loneliness of all the work-related separations if we hadn't had our cell phones. I believe in my heart the cell phone helped to draw us closer in our marriage by helping us to work through his airline career separations."[8]

Cell phones have not only improved the dynamic between husbands and wives but also between parents and children. Research conducted by Vodaphone found that 75 percent of minors (under eighteen years old) feel their relationships with their parents, siblings, and other relatives are closer thanks to their cell phones. Even more—89 percent—believe mobile technology has helped them to get along better with friends as well. "Obviously, there are plenty of ways that technology has changed our lives," writes Andreas Bernström, the chief executive officer of Rebtel, a Swedish firm that provides voice over internet protocol (VOIP) apps for cell phones. "But whereas it may have initially driven us apart, recent advances are bringing us back together, bridging the distance between families and friends and making loved ones feel closer and better connected than ever before."[9]

> "I believe in my heart the cell phone helped to draw us closer in our marriage by helping us to work through his airline career separations."[8]
>
> —Jenny Lanker, a wellness expert and the wife of an airline pilot

Personal relationships are not the only ones that have been improved by cell phones. Professional relationships have improved as well. People can send quick questions or updates via text to all kinds of professionals—teachers, professors, weight-loss counselors, therapists, members of the clergy, and even doctors. "Because of the health devices we choose to use, our . . . [doctors] are able to monitor our health conditions more closely and regularly,"[10] write technology experts Charles Levy and David Wong. These ongoing conversations with professionals promote health and well-being by keeping people involved with the care, counseling, or other help they are receiving.

Communicating with Pictures

Cell phone makers eventually equipped their smartphones with color screens, fully functional Internet browsers, media players, video games, GPS navigation, and digital cameras for taking photographs and videos. A picture is worth a thousand words, according to the old adage, and cell phone users are able to show friends and family where they are and what they are doing simply by posting photos and videos on websites like Instagram, Snapchat, Twitter, and Facebook. "We're seeing formerly 'divisive' technologies connecting older and younger generations in ways never before thought possible," writes Bernström. "It's no longer a surprise to see a mom posting a link on her daughter's Facebook wall, or . . . a grandfather sharing a YouTube video from his favorite rock 'n' roll band with his friends."[11] By posting pictures, cell phone users can tell a lot about their life to many friends and family members at once. The comments and responses such posts receive can further strengthen bonds between people. Often such comments reveal similar interests or experiences that the two people might not have known existed. These shared interests sometimes turn mere acquaintances into closer friends.

Connecting over the Internet with video-based apps like FaceTime and Skype has allowed people to communicate nonverbally as well as verbally. Communication experts say that nonverbal communication—the facial expressions and body language of both speakers and listeners—constitutes about two-thirds of communication. Video chat apps improve communication because people can see each other's faces and read their changing expressions and body language. These physical actions, known as nonverbal cues, provide additional context for the spoken words. Nonverbal cues enable the people in a video chat to detect the emotions that accompany the other person's words.

"Recent advances are bringing us back together, bridging the distance between families and friends and making loved ones feel closer and better connected than ever before."[9]

—Andreas Bernström, the chief executive officer of the communications firm Rebtel

Nonverbal communication can prevent many of the misunderstandings that sometimes occur in written and voice-only communications, improving relationships between people. "Richer, non-verbal cues detectable in face-to-face contact enable candid and quick exchange of ideas, and minimize the possibility of messages getting lost in interpretation or being wrongly decoded, thus avoiding future misunderstandings," write Levy and Wong. "For example, Corning, the manufacturer of glass and ceramics, discovered that 80 percent of their innovative ideas came from face-to-face contact."[12]

The anytime, anywhere communications capabilities of the cell phone are not just a revolution in technology. They are a revolution in human connectedness.

Cell Phones Push People Apart

"Too many of us have become slaves to the devices that were supposed to free us. . . . Instead, we're constantly bombarded by bells, buzzers and chimes that alert us to messages we feel compelled to view and respond to immediately."

—Jane E. Brody, a health columnist for the *New York Times*

Jane E. Brody, "Hooked on Our Smartphones," *New York Times*, January 9. 2017. www.nytimes.com.

Consider these questions as you read:

1. Do you agree with the perspective that more time spent on the cell phone means less time spent in face-to-face communications? Explain your answer.
2. Do you or someone you know ever use a cell phone to avoid interacting with people—and what effect does this have on relationships?
3. How persuasive is that argument that self-editing in chats and posts is a barrier to real intimacy and results in superficial interaction? Explain your answer.

Editor's note: The discussion that follows presents common arguments made in support of this perspective, reinforced by facts, quotes, and examples taken from various sources.

You see it in all kinds of public settings—trains, buses, waiting rooms, restaurants, school cafeterias—people with their heads down, staring at their cell phones, scrolling through posts or chatting with friends. Even in social situations such as meals, parties, wedding receptions, and even funerals, people are checking their cell phones. Sometimes cell phone users are actually chatting on their phones while maintaining eye contact with someone in person, a process known as phubbing (short for *phone snubbing*). Increasingly, people are withdrawing from the world around them and into the digital world of their cell phones. Most cell phone users see nothing wrong with this, but many social scientists do. Although the quantity of communications is increasing through online chats, posts, and comments, the quality is decreasing. Cell phone users edit their remarks before sending, creating online personas that are quite different than their real selves. Genuine communication is diminishing. People are drifting apart.

An Addiction to Technology

The amount of cell phone usage is astonishing. A 2017 survey by the Pew Research Center found that fully 100 percent of adults age eighteen to twenty-nine own a cell phone, with 92 percent owning smartphones. Pew also found that 73 percent of teens had access to a cell phone. According to a 2016 survey of 1,240 parents and their children, ages twelve to eighteen, conducted for Common Sense Media, nearly 80 percent of teens said they check their phones hourly; 72 percent feel the need to respond immediately. For many, it feels like an addiction. According to the survey, 50 percent of teens feel they are addicted to their mobile devices. A larger number of parents, 59 percent, said their teens were addicted. "Technological addiction can happen to anyone,"[13] says digital addiction expert Holland Haiis.

> "There is a certain amount of psychological anxiety involved with any social interaction and we can avoid that feeling by retreating into our device."[15]
>
> —Marguerite Summer, a psychologist in training

Although cell phone addiction is not yet a recognized disorder in the United States, the more time spent on the phone means less time communicating face-to-face with family and friends. "It's connections to other human beings—real-life connections, not digital ones—that nourish us and make us feel like we count," says Nancy Colier, a psychotherapist and the author of the book *The Power of Off.* "Digital communications don't result in deeper connections, in feeling loved and supported."[14]

Cell phone users are not only focusing on their devices to the exclusion of people around them, but they are also often using their devices to avoid people. A 2015 study by the Pew Research Center found that 47 percent of smartphone owners age eighteen to twenty-nine used their phone to avoid interacting with the people around them at least once during the prior week. "There is a certain amount of psychological anxiety involved with any social interaction and we can avoid that feeling by retreating into our device,"[15] says Marguerite Summer, a psychologist in training.

To be fair, this avoidance technique is not entirely new. In the past, people read books, magazines, or newspapers in public places to do the same thing. What is different is that people are now using the technique even in social settings, such as receptions or parties. "Parties used to be a nightmare for the socially awkward," writes humorist Michael Deacon, only partly tongue-in-cheek. "These days, though, there's no need to worry; just get out your phone. Before, it looked as if everyone else was shunning you; but now, it looks as if you're shunning everyone else. . . . That's what I love about smartphones. They aren't just a means of communication. They're a means of avoiding it."[16]

Barriers to Intimacy

Many cell phone users are more comfortable chatting over the phone than having face-to-face conversations. When sociologist Sherry Turkle asked a teenage boy what was wrong with conversation, he replied, "What's wrong with conversation? I'll tell you what's wrong with conversation! It takes place in real time and you can't control what you're going to say."[17] The ability to control what they say and how they appear is a major reason why people often prefer online conversations to face-to-face ones. "I spend my time online wanting to be seen as witty, intelligent, involved, and having the right ironic distance from everything," a thirty-four-year-old woman named Sharon told Turkle. "On Twitter, on Facebook, I'm geared toward showing my best self, showing me to be invulnerable or with as little vulnerability as possible."[18]

Self-editing comes at a cost, however, as some cell phone users are coming to realize. "I worry that I'm giving up the responsibility for who

Cell Phone Addiction Disrupts Relationships

Addiction—whether to drugs or gambling or cell phones—is harmful to human relationships. Addiction leads to negativity, dishonesty, and conflict and drives people apart because the addictive behavior becomes more important to the addict than relationships. This may be happening with cell phones. According to a 2016 survey of 1,240 parents and their children, ages twelve to eighteen, many young people are addicted to their cell phones. Half of the teens said they felt this to be the case—and 59 percent of parents agreed. Other results—including the high percentage of teens who say they feel they must respond immediately to messages and texts—further supports concerns about cell phone addiction and its impact on relationships.

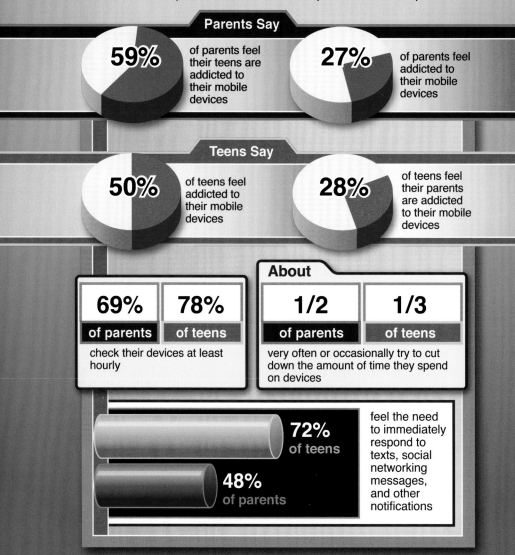

Parents Say

59% of parents feel their teens are addicted to their mobile devices

27% of parents feel addicted to their mobile devices

Teens Say

50% of teens feel addicted to their mobile devices

28% of teens feel their parents are addicted to their mobile devices

69%	**78%**
of parents	of teens

check their devices at least hourly

About

1/2	**1/3**
of parents	of teens

very often or occasionally try to cut down the amount of time they spend on devices

72% of teens

48% of parents

feel the need to immediately respond to texts, social networking messages, and other notifications

Source: Common Sense Media, "Dealing with Devices," May 3, 2016. www.commonsensemedia.org.

I am to how other people see me," says Sharon. "I'm not being rigorous about knowing my own mind, my own thoughts. You get lost in the performance."[19]

Presenting oneself in the best possible way is not new either; people have always presented themselves differently to different people, an action sometimes called wearing a social mask. But the kind of performance Sharon describes is a barrier to intimacy. She does not reveal her authentic self while chatting even to friends, so conversation can never reach any depth of understanding or emotion. People chat, but they do not get to know each other.

> "Mobile phone use temporarily decreases prosocial behavior."[20]
>
> —Ajay T. Abraham, Anastasiya Pocheptsova, and Rosellina Ferraro, researchers at the University of Maryland

Researchers have found that the mere presence of a cell phone diminishes intimacy, even when it is not being used. Researchers at the Massachusetts Institute of Technology have found that people held different face-to-face conversations when a cell phone was present and when it was not. Thinking they might be interrupted at any time, the speakers avoided deep conversations, preferring to stick to superficial topics. According to a 2015 Pew Research survey of 1,635 adults, 57 percent of smartphone owners reported feeling distracted because of their phone, and 36 percent reported that their phone made them feel frustrated.

A Loss of Empathy

Cell phones also inhibit feelings of caring and empathy, according to researchers at the University of Maryland. They found that cell phone use decreases the desire to help people, despite the fact that cell phone users feel connected to others. Ironically, it is the feeling of connectedness that leads to the more selfish behavior, according to the researchers. "Mobile phone use evokes feelings of social connectedness to other people and fulfills the need to belong or affiliate," write researchers Ajay T. Abraham, Anastasiya Pocheptsova, and Rosellina Ferraro. "This subsequently decreases the need for further affiliation and lowers concern for other people. As a consequence, mobile phone use temporarily decreases prosocial behavior."[20] The researchers found that cell phone users were less inclined to volunteer for a community service activity when asked, compared to the control-group counterparts. The cell phone users were also less persistent in solving word problems, even though they knew their answers would translate to a monetary donation to charity.

As cell phones become prevalent among young teens and tweens, teachers and counselors are noticing a lack of empathy among young people. "The kids aren't cruel," observes Ava Reade, the dean of Holbrooke School in New York. "But they are not emotionally developed. Twelve-year-olds play on the playground like eight-year-olds. The way they exclude one another is the way eight-year-olds would play. They don't seem able to put themselves in the place of other children." The lack of empathy prevents the children from bonding. "They are not developing that way of relating where they listen and learn how to look at each other and hear each other,"[21] says Reade.

Cell phone use is actually driving people apart. As one man puts it, cell phones bring their users "closer to people they're far away from, but farther from the people they're close . . . to."[22]

Chapter Two

Are Cell Phones Affecting Human Intelligence?

Cell Phones Are Harming Human Intelligence

- Cell phones encourage multitasking, which harms cognitive thinking.
- The very presence of a cell phone decreases mental focus and impairs thinking.
- Extensive cell phone use decreases memory and leads to mental laziness.

The Debate at a Glance

Cell Phones Are Enhancing Human Intelligence

- Cell phones provide access to the Internet's vast and growing capabilities and data.
- People equipped with cell phones can solve complex problems faster than people without them can.
- Cell phones are an extension of the brain in the same way that tools are an extension of the hands.

Cell Phones Are Harming Human Intelligence

"We all understand the joys of our always-wired world—the connections, the validations, the laughs . . . the info. I don't want to deny any of them here. But we are only beginning to get our minds around the costs."

—Andrew Sullivan, an author, editor, and blogger

Andrew Sullivan, "I Used to Be a Human Being," *New York Magazine*, September 18, 2016. http://nymag.com.

Consider these questions as you read:

1. Do you agree with researchers who say that multitasking—using a cell phone and doing something else at the same time—reduces the ability to focus and causes stress? Why or why not?
2. What is your view of the argument that people depend on their cell phones so much that they are losing the ability to remember things and to think for themselves?
3. Should schools allow cell phones in the classroom? Why or why not?

Editor's note: The discussion that follows presents common arguments made in support of this perspective, reinforced by facts, quotes, and examples taken from various sources.

People use their cell phones to do many things they used to do themselves—to provide directions to various destinations, to do their math, to autocorrect their spelling, and hundreds of other tasks through a multitude of apps. This raises the question: Are people becoming too reliant on their cell phones? Are they offloading too much of their thinking to their devices? Are smartphones making them dumb?

Multitasking and the Brain

A 2016 study by technology research firm Dscout found that cell phone users connect to their devices an average of 76 times a day, with heavy users averaging 132 sessions per day. Many of these sessions occur while the user is doing something else, a process known as multitasking. Clifford Nass, a professor of communications at Stanford University, believes that multitasking is at odds with how the human brain has evolved and can be detrimental to its performance. "Our brains aren't really built for that," says Nass.

> We evolved in a world in which there [were] very few things to look at at one time, or, more precisely, very few things that weren't related. So if you were out hunting an animal, yeah, you might look at a lot of things, but they were all about hunting that animal. Now what we see is people trying to use information in a totally unrelated way. And that's not how your brain, or anyone's brain, is built.[23]

As a result, cell phones are affecting the thinking of their users—in particular, the ability to prioritize and concentrate on the things that matter most. "Smartphones encourage you to do multiple things at once, which is not physiologically healthy for you because we are not built to do a multitude of tasks at one time," says Nass. "Research shows that multitasking lessens your ability to focus on what is relevant. Your phone makes you feel like you have to respond, which then increases your stress and harms your cognitive thinking."[24]

"A Brain Drain"

These distractions cause what researchers at the McCombs School of Business at the University of Texas at Austin call "a brain drain." They found that people with cell phones located nearby performed worse on cognitive tests than did subjects who did not have phones nearby. The researchers concluded that the very process of ignoring the cell phone reduces the brain's capacity to think. "Your conscious mind isn't thinking about your smartphone, but that process—the process of requiring yourself to not think about something—uses up some of your limited cognitive resources. It's a brain drain,"[25] says Adrian Ward, one of the authors of the study.

The constant bombardment of cell phone alerts for text messages and social media updates prevents cell phone users from thinking deeply, according to Sandy Chapman, the chief director for the Center for Brain Health in Dallas. She says the brain is too distracted to solve complex problems. "It's making us dumber because . . . it's really keeping us at this distracted level, so everything that we're thinking about tends to be more quick, more minute, less synthesized, and that's what's making us dumber."[26]

The brain drain might not be good for people at work, but it is horrible for students, who are being exposed to some topics and information for the first and perhaps only time. The presence of cell phones in the classroom has the potential for inflicting permanent damage because students will miss learning opportunities they might never have again, such as learning algebra or studying a foreign language. Cell phones are disrupting learning and preventing a deeper knowledge of the world. "The variance in student ability to focus and engage in the actual task at hand is disconcerting," says Rob Redies, a chemistry teacher at Fern Creek High School in Louisville, Kentucky, discussing cell phones in the classroom. "Although technology and the wealth of information that it can provide has the potential to shrink achievement gaps, I am actually seeing the opposite take place within my classroom."[27]

> "Your phone makes you feel like you have to respond, which then increases your stress and harms your cognitive thinking."[24]
>
> —Clifford Nass, a professor of communications at Stanford University

The entertainment features of cell phones actually increase the divide between low and high achievers, according to Paul Barnwell, an English teacher at Fern Creek. He writes, "Struggling students (from all backgrounds) seem to be more susceptible than their higher-achieving peers to using their smartphones for noneducational purposes while in school."[28]

Cell Phones Are a Huge Distraction in College Classrooms

According to a 2016 study, almost 97 percent of college students use their cell phones during class for reasons that have nothing to do with education. The problem with this is obvious: Students are not paying attention to class lectures, which means they are missing out on important instruction and are not learning. The most common cell phone–related distraction, according to the study, is texting—with e-mail and social networking not far behind. The study, done by a researcher at the University of Nebraska, Lincoln, involved 675 undergraduate and graduate students (ages eighteen to twenty-two) in twenty-six states.

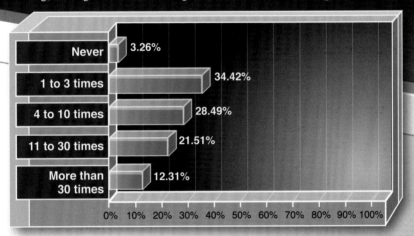

On a typical school day, how often do you use a digital device during classes for non-classroom-related activities such as texting, talking on a smartphone, emailing, surfing the Web, tweeting, or other social networking?

Never	3.26%
1 to 3 times	34.42%
4 to 10 times	28.49%
11 to 30 times	21.51%
More than 30 times	12.31%

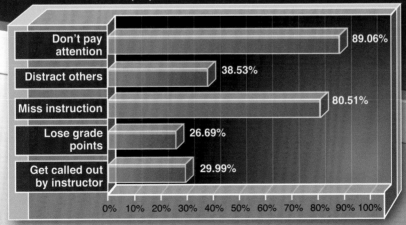

What are the three biggest disadvantages to using a digital device in the classroom for non-class purposes?

Don't pay attention	89.06%
Distract others	38.53%
Miss instruction	80.51%
Lose grade points	26.69%
Get called out by instructor	29.99%

Source: Bernard R. McCoy, "Digital Distractions in the Classroom Phase II: Student Classroom Use of Digital Devices for Non-Class Purposes," *JoME (Journal of Media Education)*, vol. 7, no. 1, January 2016. http://en.calameo.com.

Researchers at Kent State University confirm Redies's observation. They found that more daily cell phone use correlated with lower grade point averages (GPAs) of college students. The researchers surveyed 536 undergraduate students from eighty-two different majors. "Cell phone use was significantly and negatively related to actual college GPA after controlling for demographic variables,"[29] the researchers concluded.

Impaired Memory

Researchers have also found that using cell phones to store data is destroying the ability to recall information, such as important phone numbers, dates and times of important meetings, and critical dates like birthdays and anniversaries. "While earlier, we'd easily remember at least ten important phone numbers by rote, today we can't recall any other than our own," says Sangeeta Ravat, the head of the Department of Neurology at India's Seth Gordhandas Sunderdas Medical College and King Edward Memorial Hospital, who conducted the studies. "Our mind is not challenged. Everything is fed in the phonebook, and under categories—family, work, miscellaneous," says Ravat. "Our minds are getting lazy because gadgets ensure we don't use them enough."[30]

Memory is not the only mental faculty negatively affected by cell phone use, according to researchers at Waterloo University in Ontario, Canada. The devices also appear to decrease the initiative to think. In short, they are making their users lazy. In three studies involving 660 participants, the researchers tested various mental skills, such as verbal and math skills. They also looked at how the subjects thought—whether they were intuitive thinkers, who rely on gut feelings and instincts when making decisions, or analytical thinkers, who are more prone to use logic and deduction. The researchers also studied the subjects' smartphone habits. The researchers found that subjects who demonstrated stronger cognitive

> "Our research provides support for an association between heavy smartphone use and lowered intelligence."[31]
>
> —Gordon Pennycook, a researcher at Waterloo University

skills and a greater willingness to think analytically spent less time using their smartphones' search engines than the intuitive thinkers did. By contrast, the intuitive thinkers used their device's search engines rather than their own brainpower. "They may look up information that they actually know or could easily learn, but are unwilling to make the effort to actually think about it," says Gordon Pennycook, one of the lead authors of the study. "Our research provides support for an association between heavy smartphone use and lowered intelligence."[31]

Sleep Deprivation and Intelligence

Another cell phone behavior—checking the phone throughout the night—is also affecting the brain's ability to process information. "When you don't get enough sleep, one of the things that starts to happen is your ability to process information begins to stop," says Stanley Coren, a neuropsychologist formerly at the University of British Columbia in Vancouver, Canada. "You actually act as though you're losing I.Q. points. In fact, if you lose an hour of sleep below eight hours, it's the equivalent of losing one point of I.Q."[32] This is what is happening to cell phone users, according to Larry D. Rosen, a professor emeritus of psychology at California State University, Dominguez Hills. In a 2014 study of college students, Rosen found that only 2 percent of the subjects turned off their phone and put it in another room at bedtime. Another 17 percent turned it off (or placed it on silent or airplane mode) but kept it nearby. The remaining 81 percent said they left their phone with the ringer on or on vibrate and kept it next to their bed or within reach. "This was a major contributor to sleep disturbances in this study and in others and when I mention that to students they acknowledge that they are aware of the downsides but aren't going to change their behavior."[33]

Unfortunately, the same can be said for the impact of cell phones on all areas of intelligence: people are aware of the downsides, but they are not going to change their behavior. They are happy to let their machines do their thinking for them.

Cell Phones Are Enhancing Human Intelligence

"You're not Robocop and you're not Terminator, but you're cyborgs every time you look at a computer screen or use one of your cell phone devices."

—Amber Case, an anthropologist at Harvard University

Amber Case, "Are Our Devices Turning Us into a New Kind of Human?," interview by Guy Raz, *TED Radio Hour*, NPR, September 11, 2015. www.npr.org.

Consider these questions as you read:

1. What are the potential benefits and drawbacks of cell phones providing access to a unified Internet in which machines will find and provide data for users?
2. Do you agree that cell phones are an extension of the brain in the same way that tools are an extension of the hands? Why or why not?
3. Do you think a person's intelligence should be measured by itself or in partnership with a cell phone connected to the Internet? Explain your answer.

Editor's note: The discussion that follows presents common arguments made in support of this perspective, reinforced by facts, quotes, and examples taken from various sources.

Cell phones are marvelous things. Their developers have managed to load these devices with nearly every communication advance of the last two hundred years—the camera, telephone, phonograph, motion pictures, radio, television, video, and live chat. There are even apps for sending and receiving Morse code, the language of the telegraph. But cell phones are more than pocket-sized media centers. They are the user's primary access point to the most important invention of all—the Internet. Today the Internet is a collection of billions of web pages that people access manually, often by tapping their cell phone's display. In the future the Internet will be a single, unified source of data that not only responds to the users' commands—via voice or eye movement—but anticipates their needs and provides them with essential information. Accessed through the cell phone, the Internet will become an extension of the human mind, making our species more intelligent than ever before.

Connecting to the Semantic Web

Tim Berners-Lee, the Nobel Prize–winning computer scientist who developed the World Wide Web, calls this unified, proactive version of the Internet the Semantic Web. It consists of machines talking to machines to carry out a user's commands and even anticipate the user's needs. The Semantic Web will combine data from interconnected electronic sensors and devices, known as the Internet of Things, with all data on the Internet, which the machines will be able to read and interpret by themselves. In his 1999 book *Weaving the Web*, Berners-Lee described the Semantic Web:

> I have a dream for the Web . . . and it has two parts. In the first part, the Web becomes a much more powerful means for collaboration between people. . . . In the second part of the dream, collaborations extend to computers. Machines become capable of analyzing all of the data on the Web—the content, links, and transactions between people and computers. A "Semantic Web," which should make this possible, has yet to emerge, but when it does, the day-to-day mechanisms of trade, bureaucracy, and our daily lives will be handled by machines talking to machines, leaving humans to provide the inspiration and intuition.[34]

For example, an intelligent personal assistant (IPA)—such as Siri, Cortana, or Viv—could receive data from wearable sensors in a cell phone user's clothing to detect signs of hunger and then connect that with a knowledge of the user's food preferences, eating habits, GPS location,

People Will Partner with Devices to Be Smarter

A report by the Swedish communications company Ericsson found that a majority of consumers are happy to partner with devices such as smartphones to enhance their own intelligence. Ericsson surveyed more than one hundred thousand consumers across forty countries about their views on the future of technology. Seventy-three percent said they would use devices capable of artificial intelligence (AI) for search engines, 64 percent said they would use AI as a travel guide, and 57 percent said they would use AI as a personal assistant —all of which is already possible through AI-smartphone interfaces.

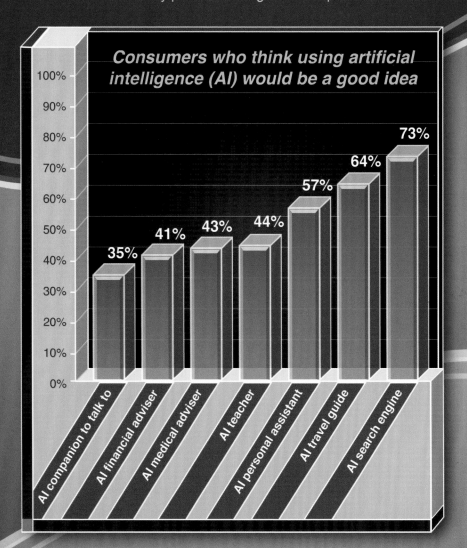

Consumers who think using artificial intelligence (AI) would be a good idea

Category	Percent
AI companion to talk to	35%
AI financial adviser	41%
AI medical adviser	43%
AI teacher	44%
AI personal assistant	57%
AI travel guide	64%
AI search engine	73%

Source: ConsumerLab, "10 Hot Consumer Trends 2016," December 2015, p. 6. www.ericsson.com.

finances, and calendar to make a suggestion: "If you are hungry, there is a noodle shop around the corner with a luncheon special of your favorite item. Your next meeting is in one hour. This is the optimum time to eat."

Answers at Warp Speed

A cell phone connected to the Semantic Web could handle intellectual tasks with equal ease. Someone writing a book about, say, cell phones, could simply say, "Give me the latest research regarding the impact of cell phones on academic performance." The IPA would connect with advanced search engines that would not only find the data but also rate it for quality by looking at things such as how many times a study has been cited by other researchers. Instead of opening page after page of search results and scanning each one for useful information, the Semantic Web user will receive curated information streamed to his or her work environment.

"We're going to use those tools to make ourselves more expressive and more intelligent."[35]

—Ray Kurzweil, futurist

This process will become so natural and fast that users will be able to focus nearly all of their energy on creative thinking and decision making. By delegating the mundane tasks to machines, human beings will function more efficiently than ever, leading to more breakthroughs and more satisfaction in their work and their lives. Average people will become like Captain Kirk in the original *Star Trek* television series, asking the starship's computer questions and giving it commands but making the key decisions himself. "We're going to use those tools to make ourselves more expressive and more intelligent,"[35] writes futurist Ray Kurzweil.

Superintelligence

This is already happening, according to Columbia law professor Tim Wu. He argues that cell phone users with access to the Internet already are outstripping highly intelligent people of the past. He constructs a thought experiment to illustrate his point:

A well-educated time traveller from 1914 enters a room divided in half by a curtain. A scientist tells him that his task is to ascertain the intelligence of whoever is on the other side of the curtain by asking whatever questions he pleases. The traveller's queries are answered by a voice with an accent that he does not recognize (twenty-first-century American English). The woman on the other side of the curtain has an extraordinary memory. She can, without much delay, recite any passage from the Bible or Shakespeare. Her arithmetic skills are astonishing—difficult problems are solved in seconds. She is also able to speak many foreign languages, though her pronunciation is odd. Most impressive, perhaps, is her ability to describe almost any part of the Earth in great detail, as though she is viewing it from the sky. . . . Our time traveller would conclude that, in the past century, the human race achieved a new level of superintelligence.[36]

The woman behind the curtain is not actually superintelligent, Wu writes, but simply "a regular human who has augmented her brain using two tools: her mobile phone and a connection to the Internet and, thus, to Web sites like Wikipedia, Google Maps, and Quora. To us, she is unremarkable, but to the man she is astonishing." At the same time, Wu concedes, the person operating the cell phone is "likely stupider than our friend from the early twentieth century, who has a longer attention span, may read and write Latin, and does arithmetic faster." Nevertheless, Wu writes, cell phones are augmenting human intelligence and will continue to do so, enabling human beings to evolve "technologically rather than biologically."[37]

The Human-Machine Partnership

Wu is not alone in this opinion. Social psychologist and technology theorist Jenny Davis suggests that intelligence should be gauged by assessing the human-machine partnership. She suggests that rather than understanding the brain and the device as separate sources of thought, scientists should consider them as a single unit, much as they do with other tools. For example, when evaluating how fast a human being can travel, we do not limit ourselves to thinking only of how fast a person can run; we consider how fast a person can travel in a car, airplane, or spaceship. "Humans' defining characteristic is our need for tools," says Davis. "Our brains literally developed with and through technology. This continues to be true. Brains are highly plastic, and new technologies change how cognition [thinking] works."[38]

One need only to look at the advent of writing and written records to see how technology already has affected human intelligence. Prior to the invention of writing, human beings created magnificent works, such as *The Epic of Gilgamesh*, *The Iliad*, and *The Odyssey*. These works were memorized and passed down from generation to generation through an oral tradition. One can imagine critics of writing suggesting that transcribing these and other works would diminish the ability to memorize, and they would have been right. But having a written record of previous works allowed later thinkers to build on the work of their predecessors in a way that the oral tradition did not allow. The achievements of William Shakespeare, Isaac Newton, and Albert Einstein would not have been possible without the existence of books and other external, nonmemorized information.

> "It isn't just a phone. I mean, through it you have access to an infinite set of ideas."[40]
>
> —Guy Raz, a journalist and radio host for NPR

Cell phones and the Internet are a new and faster way of storing, retrieving, and applying enormous amounts of information—far more than any person could know or access in even the largest of conventional libraries. "We are a human-machine civilization," says Kurzweil. "Computers are doing things all the time that we can't possibly do."[39] The cell phone is each person's connection to this vast intelligence. "It isn't just a phone," says Guy Raz, a journalist who specializes in technology. "I mean, through it you have access to an infinite set of ideas."[40]

Chapter Three

Are Cell Phones Affecting Human Health?

Cell Phones Are Improving Human Health

- Cell phone cameras, together with apps, can diagnose diseases such as skin cancer.
- Cell phones paired with wearable sensors can alert health professionals when a patient has a problem.
- Video chatting enables 24/7 long-distance medical care, known as telemedicine.

The Debate at a Glance

Cell Phones Are Harming Human Health

- Drivers and pedestrians distracted by cell phones are having deadly accidents.
- Cell phone use is shaping harmful exercise, eating, and sleeping habits.
- Heavy cell phone use is linked to increased anxiety, depression, and suicide.

Cell Phones Are Improving Human Health

"Mobile devices as small as my cell phone can perform ECGs [electrocardiograms], DIY [do-it-yourself] blood tests, or serve as a thermometer, all without even leaving my house."

—Daniel Newman, the principal analyst of Futurum Research and the chief executive officer of Broadsuite Media Group

Daniel Newman, "Top Five Digital Transformation Trends in Health Care," *Forbes*, March 7, 2017. www.forbes.com.

Consider these questions as you read:

1. If you were ill, how would you feel about a mobile app diagnosing your illness based on images from a cell phone camera? Explain your answer.
2. Would you ever consider using a health care app? If yes, under what conditions? If no, why not?
3. How do you feel about remotely conducted visits with doctors and other health care professionals? Under what circumstances, if any, would you prefer in-person interaction—and why?

Editor's note: The discussion that follows presents common arguments made in support of this perspective, reinforced by facts, quotes, and examples taken from various sources.

Today's cell phones house powerful technologies, including LED lights, high-resolution digital cameras, and powerful computer processors that enable them to perform important health care tasks. Software engineers are harnessing these technologies to provide a wide array of health care services that are improving the health of cell phone users and their families. In addition, cell phones allow health care professionals and patients to communicate instantly and efficiently. Because of these advances, cell phones are improving health now and will continue to do so with even greater effectiveness in the future.

Identifying Skin Cancer

Cell phones have not found a cure for cancer, but they can identify some forms of it. Apple's SkinVision skin cancer risk app uses fractal geometry to analyze cell phone images to see if the photographs contain telltale signs of skin cancer. In a 2015 study published in the *Journal of the European Academy of Dermatology and Venereology*, SkinVision was used to scan 195 skin images. It correctly diagnosed 73 percent of the images that showed cancerous tissue. It also correctly identified 83 percent of images depicting tissue that was not cancerous. (Doctors shown the same images correctly identified 88 percent of the cancerous images and 97 percent of those that were not cancerous.) The SkinVision website states that so far the app has assessed more than 2.5 million skin pictures and detected more than 1,100 cancerous skin lesions.

One of those belonged to Nikie Duddridge, a forty-six-year-old woman from Cannington, Somerset, England. She used SkinVision to scan suspicious moles on her body. "The app soon told me that most of the moles on my arms and legs were completely normal," she wrote in August 2017. "But when I scanned the one on my ankle—about half the size of a fingernail—the app gave a 'red warning' sign and advised that I get immediate medical attention." Her doctor took one look at the mole and ordered a biopsy, a test to determine whether a tissue is cancerous. The biopsy revealed that not only was the mole skin cancer but also that Duddridge had a fist-sized tumor behind it. "I was shocked and terrified," said Duddridge. However, thanks to the early detection, Duddridge's doctors were able

"When I scanned the [mole] on my ankle—about half the size of a fingernail—the app gave a 'red warning' sign and advised that I get immediate medical attention."[41]

—Nikie Duddridge, a user of the SkinVision cancer detection app for cell phones to provide successful treatment. "Luckily, because the cancer was caught in time, the surgeon managed to get everything out and I was given the all-clear with no need for further treatment,"[41] she said.

Accurate Measurements at Home

The cell phone camera can be used to perform all kinds of tests and measurements. For example, cell phone images are used to measure the distances people can move their limbs and joints, known as range of motion. These measurements are important for tracking the progress of patients undergoing physical therapy after surgery or an injury. In July 2017 researchers at the University of Centro-Oeste in Guarapuava, Paraná, Brazil, compared range-of-motion measurements using a traditional mechanical device known as a universal goniometer and a smartphone app. The researchers tested thirty-four healthy women with limited range of motion in their knees. The researchers found little variation in the results from the two devices. "Measurements obtained using the smartphone goniometric application are as reliable as those of a universal goniometer," they wrote. "This application is therefore a useful tool for the evaluation of knee range of motion."[42]

Good health is more than skin deep, and researchers have found a way to use the cell phone's bright LED light and digital camera to look beneath the skin's surface to detect a range of conditions. Cell phone cameras can detect changes in the volume of blood in the tiny blood vessels beneath the surface of the skin, using a process known as photoplethysmography. These changes in blood volume occur many times a minute due to the beating of the heart. Not surprisingly, software developers have used this process to create apps that measure the user's heart rate. In 2017 researchers at the University of Udine in Italy tested the effectiveness of three of the most downloaded apps for measuring heart rate on both Android and Apple cell phones during periods of both exercise and rest. Ten young adult volunteers (four males and six females) were monitored over three days. The researchers took a total of 1,080 heart rate measurements. They compared the cell phone measurements to those taken at the same time on the same subjects using

Medical Apps Empower Ordinary People

Medical apps (easily downloaded on smartphones and often free) are giving people greater control of their health and their health care than ever before. Millions of people are downloading apps on a wide array of health issues. These apps empower ordinary people by giving them more knowledge and more say in the medical decisions that directly affect their lives.

Most Popular Types of Medical Apps Downloaded by Users

Weight loss (50 million)

Exercise (26.5 million)

Women's health (10.5 million)

Sleep and meditation (8 million)

Pregnancy (7.5 million)

Tools and instruments (6 million)

Other (18 million)

Source: Mark Schenker, "The Future of Healthcare: How Mobile Medical Apps Give Control Back to Us," Y Media Labs, January 18, 2017. https://ymedialabs.com.

a belt heart rate monitor with a precision of plus or minus 1 percent. They found that the results of the two methods were virtually the same. "All correlations appear high and statistically significant,"[43] wrote the researchers. Accurate heart rate measurement is important for those involved with physical fitness but also can be used by those with heart conditions.

Connecting to Health Devices and Sensors

Some medical device companies are developing equipment that can be plugged into a cell phone's USB port to take additional measurements. The data from these tests are processed by the cell phone app and then sent to the health care professional in charge of the patient's care. For example, researchers at Cornell University in Ithaca, New York, have developed a mobile platform for diagnosing iron deficiency called iron-Phone. It consists of a smartphone, an accessory, an app, and a disposable test strip to measure the amount of iron in the blood. The researchers collected finger-prick blood samples from twenty participants and tested them with ironPhone and standard laboratory equipment. The researchers found a high correlation in the test results from both devices, "with a sensitivity of over 90% for predicting ID (iron deficiency) via the ironPhone, demonstrating its promise for iron status assessment at the point-of-care."[44]

Cell phones can also be paired with wearable sensors to assess a patient's condition. For example, sensors that measure the inertia of a user's movements can detect when a person falls. These fall detection systems use the cell phone's communication ability to notify caregivers or relatives when a person has fallen. According to the Centers for Disease Control and Prevention, twenty-seven thousand older Americans die from falls each year: "Every second of every day in the United States an older adult falls, making falls the number one cause of injuries and deaths from injury among older Americans."[45] By notifying caregivers as soon as a fall takes place, cell phone–based fall detection systems can save thousands of lives a year.

Cell phone apps can improve health even when the data comes from the user rather than sophisticated diagnostic equipment. Apps designed to help people lose weight, control diabetes, monitor fertility, manage asthma, and many other health functions often depend on input from the user, but they have been proven effective by clinical research.

Telemedicine

Health care professionals can communicate with patients by calling, texting, using video apps, and viewing cell phone pictures, a process known as telemedicine. More than 15 million Americans received medical care remotely in 2016, according to the American Telemedicine Association. Receiving remote care is less expensive than a visit to the doctor's office. The *Wall Street Journal* reports that treating nonemergency issues such as colds, flu, earaches, and skin rashes costs around $45, compared with approximately $100 at a doctor's office. Telemedicine is highly accurate. A study by the Rambam Healthcare Campus in Haifa, Israel, found "near perfect agreement"[46] between interpretations of the X-rays viewed on smartphones compared to those viewed on traditional equipment. "Cell phones in the not too distant future will create an entirely new diagnostic system for psychiatry and physicians, providing better healthcare for millions of patients,"[47] says Mark Terranova, executive director of Restoration House, a program for convicted felons with psychiatric and substance abuse histories.

> "Cell phones in the not too distant future will create an entirely new diagnostic system for psychiatry and physicians, providing better healthcare for millions of patients."[47]
>
> —Mark Terranova, the executive director of Restoration House, a substance abuse prevention and treatment organization in Seaside, Oregon

By enabling on-demand, 24/7 care from medical professionals and interactive apps, cell phones are at the leading edge of a health care revolution. That revolution is improving health and saving lives at lower costs and with greater availability than ever before.

Cell Phones Are Harming Human Health

"It's not an exaggeration to describe iGen [people born between 1995 and 2012] as being on the brink of the worst mental-health crisis in decades. Much of this deterioration can be traced to their phones."

—Jean M. Twenge, a psychology professor at San Diego State University

Jean M. Twenge, "Have Smartphones Destroyed a Generation?," *Atlantic*, September 2017. www.theatlantic.com.

Consider these questions as you read:

1. What do you think of the analogy that cell phones are like sports cars, alluring but dangerous? Explain your answer.
2. Because research shows that having cell phones in the bedroom leads to sleep deprivation, are parents justified in banning cell phones from their kids' bedrooms at night? Explain your answer.
3. How do you feel after you post something on social media? Do you ever feel anxious about your post or about the number of likes you receive?

Editor's note: The discussion that follows presents common arguments made in support of this perspective, reinforced by facts, quotes, and examples taken from various sources.

Cell phones are like fast, shiny sports cars: the thing that makes them alluring also makes them dangerous. Cell phones offer a portal to a virtual world that for many people is more exciting than the physical one. The problem is that the cell phone users' bodies reside in the physical world, and they are being neglected. Intense cell phone use is depriving the users of exercise, affecting their eating habits, disrupting their sleep, and

Cell Phones Feature Prominently in Fatal Crashes

Cell phones are a scourge on the road. According to a 2017 government analysis, 10 percent of fatal crashes, 15 percent of injury crashes, and 14 percent of motor vehicle crashes reported to police in 2015 involved distracted drivers. A significant percentage of those drivers were using cell phones at the time of the crash. This was especially serious among drivers between the ages of twenty and twenty-nine. Government figures show that 33 percent of drivers in this age group who were involved in fatal crashes in 2015 were on their cell phones when the crash occurred.

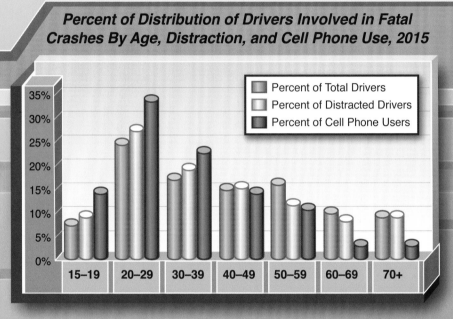

Percent of Distribution of Drivers Involved in Fatal Crashes By Age, Distraction, and Cell Phone Use, 2015

Source: National Highway Traffic Safety Administration, "Distracted Driving 2015," March 2017. www.nhtsa.gov.

causing them to be careless in dangerous situations. It also is affecting their minds in a negative way, making them anxious and depressed.

Cell Phones and Driving Do Not Mix

The ability of cell phones to distract their users is obvious and sometimes humorous. "Your primary task as a human should be being human, but when this device demands all of your attention, it can interrupt other primary tasks," writes Harvard anthropologist Amber Case; "for instance, driving or just walking down the street. I mean, we saw the video of the guy who was walking down the street texting and ran into a bear,"[48] Case adds, referring to a video taken from a news helicopter in La Crescenta, California, that went viral in 2012. Unfortunately, such distractions can also be lethal. After steadily declining over the last four decades, highway fatalities surged to the largest annual percentage increase in fifty years in 2015, according to the National Highway Traffic Safety Administration, and fatalities were even higher in 2016. Much of the increase was attributable to distracted driving, specifically from cell phone use. Scientists at Carnegie Mellon University have used brain imaging to study drivers. They found that simply listening to a cell phone

> "Drivers need to keep not only their hands on the wheel, they also have to keep their brains on the road."[49]
>
> —Marcel Just, the director of Carnegie Mellon's Center for Cognitive Brain Imaging

call reduces the amount of brain activity associated with driving by 37 percent, even when using hands-free cell phones. "Drivers need to keep not only their hands on the wheel, they also have to keep their brains on the road,"[49] said Marcel Just, director of Carnegie Mellon's Center for Cognitive Brain Imaging.

Pedestrians also run the risk of getting hurt because of cell phone use, according to a study by researchers at the University of Washington. They observed 1,102 pedestrians and found that 29.8 percent performed at least one distracting activity while crossing the street. Texting pedestrians were 3.9 times more likely than undistracted pedestrians to display at least one unsafe crossing behavior, such as disobeying the lights or failing to look both ways.

A Risk Factor for Obesity

Absorption into the virtual world is also negatively affecting cell phone users' diets and exercise regimens. Researchers at the Harvard T.H. Chan School of Public Health in Boston, Massachusetts, analyzed the results of a national survey of 24,800 US high school students who answered questions about their health behaviors. About 20 percent of the respondents used cell phones and other screen devices more than five hours a day. The researchers found such usage was associated with high consumption of sugar-sweetened beverages, less physical activity, and inadequate sleep. According to the researchers, "Using smartphones, tablets, computers, and videogames is associated with several obesity risk factors."[50]

Cell Phones and Sleep Deprivation

Inadequate sleep caused by cell phone use affects more than obesity rates; it also is linked to mental health issues such as changes in performance at school and mood disorders. Three scientists at Réseau-Morphée, a sleep clinic in Garches, France, studied the sleep habits of 786 teens (408 females and 368 males) in 2017. They found that more than 98 percent of the teens had Internet access in their bedrooms, 85 percent had cell phones, and 42 percent had a personal computer. More than half (51.7 percent) regularly used their electronic devices after bedtime. During the night, some teens woke up to continue screen-based activities: 6.1 percent played online video games, 15.3 percent sent texts, and 11 percent used social media. Teenagers who were deprived of sleep were more likely to fight sleepiness during the day and had less energy. Sleep deprivation also affected the teens' moods, with sleep-deprived teenagers reporting greater irritability and feelings of sadness. "Access to social media and especially a cell phone in teenagers' bedrooms is associated with a reduction in sleep time during the school week with negative effects on daily functioning and mood which increases with increasing age,"[51] concluded the researchers.

Australian researchers came to the same conclusion in a separate study of 1,101 students (628 females and 473 males) between the ages of thirteen and sixteen. "Increased night-time mobile phone use was directly associated with increased externalizing behavior [acting out] and decreased self-esteem and coping,"[52] wrote the researchers. Lead researcher Lynette Vernon of Murdoch University in Perth further explained that "the outcomes of not coping—lower self-esteem, feeling moody, externalising behaviours and less self-regulation [self-control], aggressive and delinquent behaviours—the levels increase as sleep problems increased."[53]

A Mental Health Crisis

Important as it is, sleep deprivation is only one aspect of cell phone use that is having a negative effect on the mental health of cell phone users. The Monitoring the Future survey, funded by the US government, found that teens who spend more time than average on screen activities are more likely to be unhappy than those who spend less time on those activities. For example, eighth-graders who spend six to nine hours a week on social media are 47 percent more likely to say they are unhappy than those who devote less time to social media, and those who spend ten or more hours a week on social media are 56 percent more likely to say they are unhappy than those who use social media less. The same pattern extends to depression and suicide. Eighth-graders who are heavy users of social media increase their risk of depression by 27 percent, and teens who spend three hours a day or more on electronic devices are 35 percent more likely to have a risk factor for suicide, such as making a suicide plan. "Rates of teen depression and suicide have skyrocketed since 2011,"[54] writes Jean M. Twenge, a psychology professor at San Diego State University.

Twenge believes that cell phones and social media are a common source of anxiety for teens. "Social media levy a psychic tax on the teen doing the posting as well, as she anxiously awaits the affirmation of comments and likes," writes Twenge. "When [research subject] Athena posts pictures to Instagram, she told me, 'I'm nervous about what people think and are going to say. It sometimes bugs me when I don't get a certain amount of likes on a picture.'" That anxiety is more intense for girls than for boys, and it translates into worse mental health. Boys' depressive symptoms increased by 21 percent from 2012 to 2015, and girls' increased by 50 percent. "The rise in suicide, too, is more pronounced among girls," writes

> "I am seeing the evidence in the numbers of depressive, anorexic, cutting children who come to see me. And it always has something to do with the computer, the Internet and the smartphone."[56]
>
> —Julie Lynn Evans, a child psychotherapist in Somerset, England

Twenge. "Although the rate increased for both sexes, three times as many 12-to-14-year-old girls killed themselves in 2015 as in 2007, compared with twice as many boys."[55]

The link between suicide and heavy cell phone use is a global phenomenon. "In the 1990s, I would have had one or two attempted suicides a year," says child psychotherapist Julie Lynn Evans in Somerset, England. "Now, I could have as many as four a month." Evans's workload is overwhelming, but when she tries to refer patients to others, they are overloaded as well. "We are all saying the same thing. There has been an explosion in numbers in mental health problems amongst youngsters." Government health statistics for the United Kingdom confirm her observation. The number of emergency admissions to child psychiatric wards had doubled in four years, and those young adults hospitalized for self-harm have increased by 70 percent in the last decade. "Something is clearly happening," says Evans, "because I am seeing the evidence in the numbers of depressive, anorexic, cutting children who come to see me. And it always has something to do with the computer, the Internet and the smartphone."[56]

Cell phones are powerful devices that can have profound effects on the moods, attitudes, and behavior of their users. They should come with a warning label: These devices can be harmful to your health.

Chapter Four

Are Cell Phones Impacting Efficiency?

Cell Phones Waste Time

- Personal cell phone use, such as social networking, decreases worker productivity.
- Personal cell phone use, such as texting and entertainment, disrupts education.
- Cell phones decrease the amount of time people spend in self-reflection and pure thinking.

The Debate at a Glance

Cell Phones Save Time

- Cell phones save time driving, calling, and faxing for people who work outside of offices.
- Cell phone apps increase productivity and collaboration among office workers.
- Cell phone apps for weather, traffic, and much more save time in personal lives.

Cell Phones Waste Time

"The average office employee spends 56 minutes per day using their cell phone at work for non-work activity. That's 43% more than the 39 minutes most managers said they thought occurred. That works out to just under five hours per week of goofing off on phones."

—Chris Morris, business writer for *Fortune*

Chris Morris, "Here's How You're Wasting 8 Hours Per Work Week," *Fortune*, July 25, 2017. http://fortune.com.

Consider these questions as you read:

1. How persuasive is the argument that automatic, habitual use of a cell phone signifies wasted time? Explain your answer.
2. Do you think schools should allow—or even encourage—students to use their cell phones in class for research and assignments? Why or why not?
3. Do you agree with the view that using cell phones in downtime prevents self-reflection and daydreaming and thus represents wasted time? Why or why not?

Editor's note: The discussion that follows presents common arguments made in support of this perspective, reinforced by facts, quotes, and examples taken from various sources.

Given the choice between doing something hard and doing something fun, most people will opt for fun. For this reason, workplaces and schools traditionally have banned radios and television and have limited personal conversations and socializing. To be productive, people must focus on the task at hand. The same is true at home. People are most productive if they do their work in a quiet place away from distractions.

52

Today this includes being removed from the pocket-sized media center we call the cell phone. Research shows that the cell phone is the greatest distraction—and the greatest time waster—ever devised.

Automatic Behaviors

In 2014 researchers at the Helsinki Institute for Information Technology in Finland asked twelve cell phone users to record all their experiences related to the use of their devices over a two-week period. The researchers found that although the users saved time by performing some tasks, such as reading their e-mails on the go, they also wasted a lot of time by playing games during lectures or surfing the Internet while at work. "While smartphones can save us time, they can also be used to waste it," says Eeva Raita, one of the authors of the study. "Killing time with a smartphone, so it seems, is quite addictive and difficult to resist. Some users reported even being embarrassed by their continuous habit of killing time, but they still could not resist it."[57]

Cell phone use is more of a habit than most users realize, according to researchers in England. They compared twenty-three participants' actual smartphone use over a two-week period with their self-reported estimates. They found that young adults used their smartphones an average of five hours a day, which was about twice as much time as participants had estimated. "The fact that we use our phones *twice* as many times as we think we do indicates that a lot of smartphone use seems to be habitual, automatic behaviors that we have no awareness of,"[58] says Sally Andrews, a psychologist at Nottingham Trent University and the lead author of the study. The hours spent in automatic, habitual use of cell phones are not productive. They can only be described as time wasted.

A Productivity Killer

Private businesses, which depend on worker productivity to earn profits, have watched the proliferation of cell phones carefully to see how they impact productivity. What they have seen are huge amounts of wasted time. A 2016 national Harris poll surveyed 2,186 human resource professionals and 3,031 full-time US workers on behalf of the recruiting firm

CareerBuilder. The poll found that 83 percent of employees have smartphones, and 82 percent of those with smartphones keep them within eye contact at work. Two out of three (66 percent) smartphone users said they access their device several times a day at work. The leading uses include personal messaging (65 percent), weather (51 percent), news (44 percent), games (24 percent), and shopping (24 percent). "While we need to be connected to devices for work, we're also a click away from alluring distractions from our personal lives like social media and various other apps,"[59] says Rosemary Haefner, the chief human resources officer at CareerBuilder.

> "While we need to be connected to devices for work, we're also a click away from alluring distractions from our personal lives like social media and various other apps."[59]
>
> —Rosemary Haefner, the chief human resources officer at CareerBuilder

Not surprisingly, when the Harris poll asked employers to rank the biggest productivity killers in the workplace, they placed cell phones and texting at the top of the list. Fully 55 percent of employers said cell phones were harming productivity—more than double the number that cited coworker interruptions (27 percent), smoking or snack breaks (27 percent), personal e-mails (26 percent), and meetings (24 percent). Three out of four employers (75 percent) reported two or more hours a day are lost in productivity because employees are distracted. "While technology helps workers stay connected while away from the office, in many cases it is causing them to disconnect while in the office, leading to a negative impact on productivity,"[60] says Ladan Nikravan, a communications manager at CareerBuilder.

A Distraction in the Classroom

Cell phones waste time in the classroom as well. Although cell phones can connect students with useful information, teens tend to shy away from academic uses. "High levels of smartphone use by teens often have a detrimental effect on achievement, because teen phone use is dominated by entertainment, not learning, applications," says Richard Freed,

Cell Phones Are the Biggest Time Wasters at Work

A Harris poll asked 2,186 human resources professionals to rank the biggest time wasters at work. Cell phone use topped the list, with 55 percent of executives citing it as a productivity killer. Two of the next three time wasters —the Internet and social media—can also be accessed via cell phones. Executives cited cell phones as a time waster more than twice as often as coworkers dropping by, smoking and snack breaks, e-mail, meetings, and noisy coworkers.

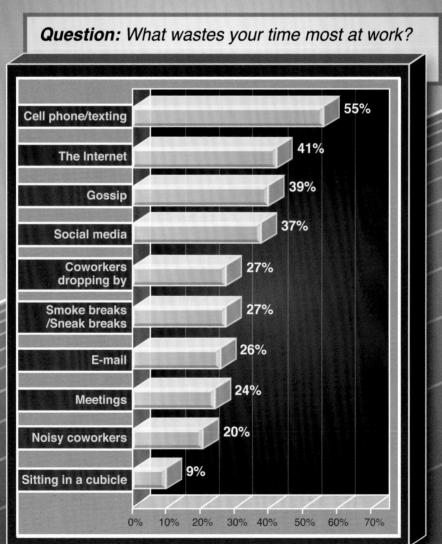

Question: What wastes your time most at work?

Cell phone/texting	55%
The Internet	41%
Gossip	39%
Social media	37%
Coworkers dropping by	27%
Smoke breaks /Sneak breaks	27%
E-mail	26%
Meetings	24%
Noisy coworkers	20%
Sitting in a cubicle	9%

0% 10% 20% 30% 40% 50% 60% 70%

Source: Ladan Nikravan, "New CareerBuilder Survey Reveals How Much Smartphones Are Sapping Productivity at Work," CareerBuilder, June 9, 2016. www.careerbuilder.com.

a clinical psychologist and the author of *Wired Child: Reclaiming Childhood in a Digital Age*. Some schools have adopted a bring-your-own-device (BYOD) policy that allows students to use their cell phones in class to enhance their learning opportunities. Brianna Crowley, a teacher who is an advocate of BYOD and cell phone use for learning, finds that while high-achieving students sometimes benefit from the BYOD program, often students who struggle academically also struggle to connect cell phone use with academic success. "Many students who may perform poorly on academic measures seem to see their devices as useful for a narrow range of tasks—most of which involve passive consuming of entertainment or knowledge-level content,"[61] she says.

Wasted Time at Home

Cell phones also make people less productive when they are away from work and school, according to John C. Dvorak, a columnist for PCMag .com. "In the old days when people were standing in line or otherwise waiting for something, they'd read a book or knit or meditate. Now they fool around on the phone," Dvorak writes. "They play games, sort messages, look for new apps. In other words, they waste time. Really, the iPhone is only the greatest handset around because it has more ways to waste time than any phone, ever."[62]

> "My smartphone does save time. But wasted time easily outweighs the saved."[63]
>
> —Taylor Martin, the managing editor of PhoneDog

Taylor Martin, the managing editor of PhoneDog, a mobile technology website, decided to take a close look at his cell phone use after he realized that he had stopped using his computer for most tasks and was spending increasing amounts of time on his mobile device. What he found surprised him enough to blog about it. "Anywhere from four to five hours, collectively, goes into social media alone," writes Martin. "After I finish working for the day, my usage ramps up. I begin scouring Android Market and App Store for more apps that I can waste my money on." Martin found that his cell phone saved him some time with such things as online shopping, looking things up, and making restaurant reservations. "My smartphone *does* save time," he concluded. "But wasted time easily outweighs the saved."[63]

A Threat to Self-Reflection

The habit of using a cell phone during periods of downtime is wasting another precious resource: downtime. People are spending less time just sitting and doing nothing—periods that can lead to self-reflection, day-dreaming, or inspiration. "What I'm really worried about is that people aren't taking time for mental reflection anymore and that they aren't slowing down and stopping," says anthropologist Amber Case. "They're not just sitting there. And really, when you have no external input, that is the time when there's a creation of self, when you can try and figure out who you really are."[64]

Sociologist Sherry Turkle shares the concern. She believes solitude is essential for self-reflection, which strengthens a person's identity and allows a person to formulate his or her own thoughts and beliefs. The stronger sense of self makes it easier to connect more deeply to other people and to appreciate what they are going through in their lives. These connections, in turn, allow for greater self-discovery. "In solitude we find ourselves," Turkle writes. "Solitude reinforces a secure sense of self, and with that, the capacity for empathy. Then conversation with others provides rich material for self-reflection. Just as alone we prepare to talk together, together we learn how to engage in more productive solitude. Technology disrupts this virtuous circle."[65] And that, perhaps, is the greatest waste of all.

Cell Phones Save Time

"Smartphones are no longer regarded as revolutionary gadgets. Instead, they're viewed as necessary tools."

—Larry Alton, *Forbes* contributor

Larry Alton, "One Decade Later: Are Smartphones All Good for the Workplace?," *Forbes*, June 22, 2017. www.forbes.com.

Consider these questions as you read:

1. Do you agree with the view that cell phones are huge time-savers? Why or why not?
2. Have you ever used a cell phone to collaborate with someone on an assignment? Did it save time or waste time? Explain.
3. What types of apps have you used that saved you time—and in what ways? What types of apps have you used that wasted your time—and in what ways?

Editor's note: The discussion that follows presents common arguments made in support of this perspective, reinforced by facts, quotes, and examples taken from various sources.

More than 40 percent of the US population was born since the advent of commercially available mobile phones. As a result, people under age thirty can hardly conceive of the amount of time people have saved thanks to their cell phones. One such person is Andrew Chapman, the founder of Social Motion Publishing in Herndon, Virginia. During a recent interview, Chapman recalled a time when he was in his car and received a text message from a prospective business partner relating to a meeting that afternoon. Confused, Chapman checked his cell phone calendar and realized the meeting was in two hours. "I had none of my materials with me," he recalls, "and I was wearing shorts and a t-shirt!" With no time to drive home, he used his cell phone to find a nearby men's clothing store, a

FedEx office to print the materials, and directions to the meeting location. He got there with ten minutes to spare. "All of that resulted in my landing the partnership with one of the top nonprofits in the US,"[66] he says.

Saving Time Outside the Office

Texting, calendars, and navigation are just some of the ways cell phones can save time. "I use my phone for an alarm that is set daily to remind me to close the parts orders on time," says Amanda McGovern, a warranty processor at Hudson's Appliance in Paradise, California. "If I miss the deadline, it could irritate customers."[67] Even the cell phone's camera is a time-saver. Its high-resolution imaging capabilities turn it into a pocket-sized document scanner. In many industries, such as printing, a customer's job cannot be started without a signed work order. With a smartphone, a sales representative can take a photo of a signed order and send it via e-mail or text to initiate a job, saving the time of driving the document to the office or sending it via fax machine.

The camera saves enormous amounts of time in the building trades as well. Instead of calling suppliers and ordering items by serial number or by trying to describe the hardware, contractors can simply take a picture of what they need and send it in a text message. "I could (and often did) take a picture of an item and send it to my supplier, asking, 'Hey can you match this doorknob?' Or whatever it was. Great time-saver,"[68] says Mike Barnett, a general contractor with the Original Imagebuilders in Central Point, Oregon.

Boosting Productivity

The time-saving capabilities of cell phones have been tracked closely among people who work in offices. A Harris poll conducted for the workforce management provider ClickSoftware found that 97 percent of the 971 respondents said apps save them time every day. The respondents estimated that their top three apps saved them 88 minutes a day. That adds up to 10 hours per week or 535 hours (22 days) per year. "The smartphone can afford its owner, on average, more than 500 hours per

The Many Ways Cell Phones Save Time

Research firm Frost & Sullivan surveyed five hundred employees of organizations with one hundred employees or more and asked them to describe how cell phones saved time on the job. Forty-six percent said the devices aided with the speed of innovation; 39 percent said they improved collaboration and productivity; 35 percent said they improved work quality; 34 percent said they reduced wasted meetings; 32 percent said they improved work accuracy.

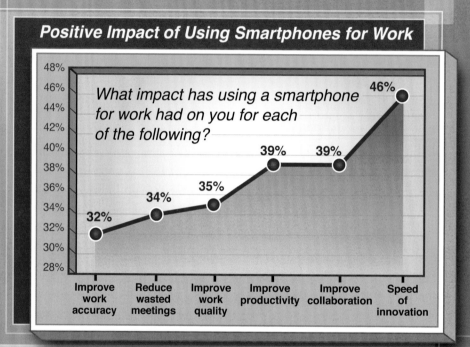

Positive Impact of Using Smartphones for Work

What impact has using a smartphone for work had on you for each of the following?

Source: Frost & Sullivan, "The Smartphone Productivity Effect: Quantifying the Productivity Gains of Smartphones in the Enterprise," August 2016, p. 7. https://static.ziftsolutions.com.

year in savings accrued by using popular apps like email, text and GPS as tallied from our survey data,"[69] says Gil Bouhnick, the vice president of ClickSoftware.

Research conducted in June and July 2016 by the research firm Frost & Sullivan found similar results. The researchers surveyed five hundred employees of organizations with one hundred employees or more.

Respondents report that as a result of using smartphones, they save fifty-eight minutes of work time each day and see an estimated productivity increase of 34 percent. The users say their devices make them more productive in several ways: Forty-two percent say smartphones help increase the speed of innovation; 41 percent say the devices give them greater flexibility; 39 percent say they improve the quality of collaboration; 39 percent also say they boost productivity; and 35 percent see an improvement in the quality of their work. "As a project manager, I'm not just responsible for meeting my timeline, but all team members' timelines," says Ci Ci Cooper, a marketing executive with a manufacturer of consumer goods in Minneapolis, Minnesota. "When I'm out of the office, I receive e-mails via cell phone regarding potential risks. Using my cell phone, I'm able to communicate with team members to get the project on track and mitigate the risk. Having a smartphone for business is a critical part of being effective at your job."[70]

> "Having a smartphone for business is a critical part of being effective at your job."[70]
>
> —Ci Ci Cooper, an executive with General Mills

Fostering Collaboration

Many cell phone apps have been developed that allow people to work on the same project and share their thoughts in real time. These collaboration apps save time compared to routing projects via e-mail, having people comment on them separately, and then trying to include everyone's ideas into one up-to-date document or report. David Levine, the chief investment officer for Artivest, an investment firm located in New York, uses the mobile app Quip for real-time collaboration. Quip allows anyone working on a project to make changes and add comments that everyone can see in a Facebook-style news feed. While riding the subway to a meeting in 2013, Levine created a blog post on his cell phone and used Quip to share it with his colleagues in New York and with freelancers in Boston and on the Greek island of Crete. The app synchronized everyone's contributions, so they were all working on the same version at the same time.

"By the time I got out of the subway, the post was done," Levine said, "and by the time I got out of the meeting, it was on the website."[71]

Streamlining Disaster Response

Cell phones can save valuable time during emergencies as well. "Cell phones have been a godsend in natural disasters when the cell networks were still up and running when land lines were down,"[72] says Karen Dall, a client service manager for Verizon Communications in Los Angeles. Cell phones can save first responders vital minutes and hours.

When rain from Hurricane Harvey caused extensive flooding in Houston, Texas, in August 2017, thousands of stranded residents used their cell phones to call for assistance. With more than a dozen emergency call centers knocked out by the storm, many flood victims could not reach 911, so they used their cell phones to ask for help on social networking sites such as Twitter, Nextdoor, and Facebook. A Facebook user group, Hurricane Harvey 2017—Together We Will Make It, was launched to help coordinate rescue efforts. "When you see that somebody has posted that they're on their roof with their one-, three- and four-year-olds and the water's up to the roof line, you have to be willing to make that phone call for them,"[73] said Annie Swinford, an unofficial volunteer who joined the Hurricane Harvey Facebook group.

> "Cell phones have been a godsend in natural disasters when the cell networks were still up and running when land lines were down."[72]
>
> —Karen Dall, a client service manager for Verizon Communications

The number of social networking posts during a disaster can be enormous, so software engineers have created computer programs to sift through the data to assist first responders. For example, when an earthquake measuring 7.8 on the Richter scale struck the mountainous nation of Nepal on April 25, 2015, data scientist Patrick Meier used his disaster response platform to collect, identify, and classify social media messages posted via cell phone by people in the disaster area. Meier and his team plotted the locations of the most urgent posts on so-called crisis maps and then provided the maps to relief agencies. "Within 24 hours of the first tremors in Nepal . . . we had the opportunity to put together live crisis maps of the most affected areas and then feed these to several relief agencies before they had even arrived," said Meier. "This meant that responders had a good picture of the areas that had received the worst of the damage before they had even touched down in [the capital] Kathmandu."[74]

Mobile apps also save time at home. Respondents to the Frost & Sullivan survey said that cell phone apps saved fifty-eight minutes a day in their personal lives. The respondents cited apps for the weather, driving directions, traffic updates, and online shopping as the biggest time-savers. When a person is trying to save time, a cell phone can help.

Source Notes

Overview: Cell Phones Are Changing the World

1. Quoted in Chelsea Stone, "Woman Falls from Foresthill Bridge, California's Highest, While Taking a Selfie," *Conde Nast Traveler*, April 6, 2017. www.cntraveler.com.
2. Quoted in Matt Villano, "Honolulu Is First City to Ban Pedestrian Texting in a Crosswalk," *Afar*, August 4, 2017. www.afar.com.
3. Christina Bonnington, "In Less than Two Years, a Smartphone Could Be Your Only Computer," *Wired*, February 10, 2015. www.wired.com.
4. Quoted in Bonnington, "In Less than Two Years, a Smartphone Could Be Your Only Computer."
5. Amber Case, "Are Our Devices Turning Us into a New Kind of Human?," interview by Guy Raz, *TED Radio Hour*, NPR, September 11, 2015. www.npr.org.
6. Quoted in Yo Zushi, "Life with a Smartphone Is Like Having a Second Brain in Your Pocket," *New Statesman*, February 22, 2017. www.newstatesman.com.
7. Tim Wu, "If a Time Traveller Saw a Smartphone," *New Yorker*, January 10, 2014. www.newyorker.com.

Chapter One: Are Cell Phones Affecting Human Relationships?

8. Jenny Lanker, interview with the author, August 22, 2017.
9. Andreas Bernström, "How Communications Technology Brings Generations Together Like Never Before," *Huffington Post*, June 13, 2013. www.huffingtonpost.com.
10. Charles Levy and David Wong, "How Smart Tech Is Improving Our Human Relationships," TechRadar Pro, July 18, 2014. www.techradar.com.
11. Bernström, "How Communications Technology Brings Generations Together Like Never Before."
12. Levy and Wong, "How Smart Tech Is Improving Our Human Relationships."
13. Quoted in Kelly Wallace, "Half of Teens Think They're Addicted to Their Smartphones," CNN, July 29, 2016. http://edition.cnn.com.
14. Quoted in Jane E. Brody, "Hooked on Our Smartphones," *New York Times*, January 9, 2017. www.nytimes.com.
15. Quoted in Elizabeth Segran, "The Case Against Smartphones," *Fast Company*, August 15, 2014. www.fastcompany.com.

16. Michael Deacon, "Of Course Smartphones Are Antisocial. That's Why We Like Them," *Telegraph*, April 15, 2016. www.telegraph.co.uk.
17. Quoted in Sherry Turkle, *Reclaiming Conversation: The Power of Talk in a Digital Age*. New York: Penguin, 2015, p. 22.
18. Quoted in Turkle, *Reclaiming Conversation,* p. 24.
19. Quoted in Turkle, *Reclaiming Conversation*, p. 24.
20. Ajay T. Abraham et al, "The Effect of Mobile Phone Use on Prosocial Behavior," ResearchGate. www.researchgate.net.
21. Quoted in Turkle, *Reclaiming Conversation*, pp. 5–6.
22. Quoted in Fatma Zakaria, "Does Social Media Bring Us Closer Together or Further Apart?," Social Clinic, March 16, 2015. www.thesocialclinic.com.

Chapter Two: Are Cell Phones Affecting Human Intelligence?

23. *Frontline*, "Interview: Clifford Nass," February 2, 2010. www.pbs.org.
24. Quoted in Julie Croteau, "Smartphone Users: Beware," BeWell Stanford. https://bewell.stanford.edu.
25. Quoted in Christopher Bergland, "Are Smartphones Making Us Stupid?," *Athlete's Way* (blog), *Psychology Today*, June 25, 2017. www.psychologyto day.com.
26. Quoted in Deanna Dewberry, "Are Smartphones Making Us Dumb?," NBC 5–KXAS, November 10, 2012. www.nbcdfw.com.
27. Quoted in Paul Barnwell, "Do Smartphones Have a Place in the Classroom?," *Atlantic*, April 17, 2016. www.theatlantic.com.
28. Barnwell, "Do Smartphones Have a Place in the Classroom?"
29. Andrew Lepp, Jacob E. Barkley, and Aryn C. Karpinski, "The Relationship Between Cell Phone Use and Academic Performance in a Sample of U.S. College Students," *SAGE Open*, January–March 2015. http://journals .sagepub.com.
30. Quoted in Reema Gehi, "Your Smartphone Is Destroying Your Memory," *Times of India*, December 3, 2013. http://timesofindia.indiatimes.com.
31. Quoted in Waterloo University, "Reliance on Smartphones Linked to Lazy Thinking," Waterloo News, March 5, 2016. https://uwaterloo.ca.
32. Quoted in Joan Lunden, "I've Got to Get Some Sleep!," January 25, 2008. www.joanlunden.com.
33. Larry D. Rosen, "Where Do You Keep Your Smartphone?," *Rewired: The Psychology of Technology* (blog), *Psychology Today*, November 2, 2014. www .psychologytoday.com.
34. Tim Berners-Lee, *Weaving the Web*. San Francisco: Harper, 1999, pp. 157–158.
35. Quoted in Andrew Nusca, "Futurist Ray Kurzweil on Smartphones, AI, and the Human Brain," CNET, November 12, 2012. www.cnet.com.

36. Wu, "If a Time Traveller Saw a Smartphone."
37. Wu, "If a Time Traveller Saw a Smartphone."
38. Jenny Davis, "How Do Smartphones Affect Human Thought?," *Cyborgology*, March 12, 2015. https://thesocietypages.org.
39. Case, "Are Our Devices Turning Us into a New Kind of Human?"
40. Quoted in Case, "Are Our Devices Turning Us into a New Kind of Human?"

Chapter Three: Are Cell Phones Affecting Human Health?

41. Nikie Duddridge, "Grandmother Diagnoses Mole on Her Ankle as Skin Cancer After Getting 'Red Warning' from Smartphone App," *Mirror*, August 5, 2017. www.mirror.co.uk.
42. Rafael Aparecido Dos Santos et al., "Evaluation of Knee Range of Motion: Correlation Between Measurements Using a Universal Goniometer and a Smartphone Goniometric Application," *Journal of Bodywork Movement Therapy*, July 2017. www.ncbi.nlm.nih.gov.
43. Maria Parpinel et al., "Reliability of Heart Rate Mobile Apps in Young Healthy Adults: Exploratory Study and Research Directions," *Journal of Innovative Health Information*, 2017. https://hijournal.bcs.org.
44. Balaji Srinivasan et al., "IronPhone: Mobile Device-Coupled Point-of-Care Diagnostics for Assessment of Iron Status by Quantification of Serum Ferritin," *Biosensors & Bioelectronics*, July 2017. www.ncbi.nlm.nih.gov.
45. Centers for Disease Control and Prevention, "Falls Are Leading Cause of Injury and Death in Older Americans," September 22, 2016. www.cdc.gov.
46. Ido Stahl et al., "Reliability of Smartphone-Based Instant Messaging Application for Diagnosis, Classification, and Decision-Making in Pediatric Orthopedic Trauma," *Pediatric Emergency Care*, July 2017. www.ncbi.nlm.nih.gov.
47. Mark Terranova, interview with the author, August 21, 2017.
48. Quoted in Case, "Are Our Devices Turning Us into a New Kind of Human?"
49. Quoted in Carnegie Mellon University, "Cell Phone Study Sparks Action," 2013. www.cmu.edu.
50. Erica Kenney and Steven Gortmaker, "United States Adolescents' Television, Computer, Videogame, Smartphone, and Tablet Use: Associations with Sugary Drinks, Sleep, Physical Activity, and Obesity," *Journal of Pediatrics*, March 2017, p. 144. www.ncbi.nlm.nih.gov.
51. Sylvie Royant-Parola et al., "The Use of Social Media Modifies Teenagers' Sleep-Related Behavior," *L'Encephale*, June 8, 2017. www.ncbi.nlm.nih.gov.
52. Lynette Vernon et al., "Mobile Phones in the Bedroom: Trajectories of Sleep Habits and Subsequent Adolescent Psychosocial Development," *Child Development*, May 29, 2017. www.ncbi.nlm.nih.gov.

53. Quoted in Elle Hunt, "Teenagers' Sleep Quality and Mental Health at Risk over Late-Night Mobile Phone Use," *Guardian*, May 30, 2017. www.theguardian.com.
54. Jean M. Twenge, "Have Smartphones Destroyed a Generation?," *Atlantic*, September 2017. www.theatlantic.com.
55. Twenge, "Have Smartphones Destroyed a Generation?"
56. Quoted in Peter Stanford, "Are Smartphones Making Our Children Mentally Ill?," *Telegraph*, March 21, 2015. www.telegraph.co.uk.

Chapter Four: Are Cell Phones Impacting Efficiency?

57. Eeva Raita, "Smartphones Are Saving and Wasting Our Time," Aalto University School of Science, October 27, 2014. http://sci.aalto.fi.
58. Quoted in Carolyn Gregoire, "You Probably Use Your Smartphone Way More than You Think," *Huffington Post*, November 2, 2015. www.huffingtonpost.com.
59. Quoted in Ladan Nikravan, "New CareerBuilder Survey Reveals How Much Smartphones Are Sapping Productivity at Work," CareerBuilder, June 9, 2016. www.careerbuilder.com.
60. Nikravan, "New CareerBuilder Survey Reveals How Much Smartphones Are Sapping Productivity at Work."
61. Quoted in Barnwell, "Do Smartphones Have a Place in the Classroom?"
62. John C. Dvorak, "The iPhone Is Ruining the Country," PCMag.com, December 15, 2009. www.pcmag.com.
63. Taylor Martin, "Does Your Smartphone Help You Save or Waste Time?," PhoneDog, November 7, 2011. www.phonedog.com.
64. Quoted in Case, "Are Our Devices Turning Us into a New Kind of Human?"
65. Turkle, *Reclaiming Conversation*, p. 10.
66. Andrew Chapman, interview with the author, August 21, 2017.
67. Amanda McGovern, interview with the author, August 19, 2017.
68. Mike Barnett, interview with the author, August 18, 2017.
69. Quoted in ClickSoftware, "Your Smartphone Could Be Worth $12,000, New Survey Finds," Business Wire, May 21, 2013. www.businesswire.com.
70. Ci Ci Cooper, interview with the author, August 19, 2017.
71. Quoted in Ted Greenwald, "Mobile Collaboration: The Smartphone Era Is Finally Getting the Productivity Software It Needs," *MIT Technology Review*, May/June 2014. www.technologyreview.com.
72. Karen Dall, interview with the author, August 19, 2017.
73. Quoted in Lauren Silverman, "Facebook, Twitter Replace 911 Calls for Stranded in Houston," All Tech Considered, August 28, 2017. www.npr.org.
74. Quoted in *Qatar Tribune*, "QCRI's Digital Initiatives Boost Nepal Earthquake Relief Works," May 26, 2015. www.qatar-tribune.com.

Cell Phones Facts

Cell Phone Usage

- More than 4.9 billion people—about 66 percent of the world's population—use cell phones, according to the Digital in 2017 Global Overview report by We Are Social and Hootsuite.
- The number of cell phone users grew by 5 percent worldwide from February 2016 to January 2017, an increase of 222 million people, according to We Are Social and Hootsuite.
- Due to people having multiple subscriptions, the number of cell phone subscriptions exceeds the number of cell phone users—8 billion to 4.9 billion—according to GSMA Intelligence.
- According to GSMA Intelligence, the average cell phone user has 1.64 cell phone subscriptions.

Cell Phones and the Internet

- According to StatCounter, more than half of the world's Internet traffic now comes from cell phones.
- More people access the Internet via cell phones (50 percent) than via laptops and desktops (45 percent), according to StatCounter.
- StatCounter reports that Internet traffic from cell phones increased 30 percent in 2016, but traffic from desktop and laptop computers decreased 20 percent. According to We Are Social and Hootsuite, 90 percent of the world's Internet users go online via a mobile device at least some of the time.
- The total number of active mobile Internet users is 3.4 billion, according to We Are Social and Hootsuite.
- According to Global Web Index, Americans spend an average of two hours and two minutes a day browsing the Internet with a cell phone, compared to four hours and nineteen minutes a day spent browsing via computer.

Cell Phones and Social Media

- More than one-third of the world's population—2.56 billion people—access social media using a cell phone, according to We Are Social and Hootsuite.
- According to We Are Social and Hootsuite, mobile social media users grew by 30 percent in 2016, up 581 million users.
- According to GSMA Intelligence, the Asia Pacific region is home to 56 percent of the world's mobile social media users.
- According to We Are Social and Hootsuite, nearly 2.8 billion people around the world now use social media at least once a month, with more than 91 percent of them doing so via mobile devices.
- In the Asia Pacific region, 95 percent of the more than 1.5 billion people who use social media on a monthly basis access it via mobile devices—the highest ratio in the world, according to We Are Social and Hootsuite.

Cell Phones and Teens

- According to the Pew Research Center report "How Teens Hang Out and Stay in Touch with Their Closest Friends," 88 percent of all teens have a cell phone of some kind.
- Texting is the number-one way all teens get in touch with their closest friends, Pew's "How Teens Hang Out" report states.
- According to Pew's "How Teens Hang Out" report, 58 percent of teens who have access to a smartphone say texting is the most common way they get in touch with their closest friend, compared with 30 percent of teens who only have access to a basic cellphone.
- The Pew Research Center's "How Teens Hang Out" report says that 21 percent of teens with basic cell phones say they make phone calls to their closest friend as a primary mode of keeping in touch, which is double the share for smartphone users.

Related Organizations and Websites

Center for Safe and Responsible Internet Use
474 W. Twenty-Ninth Ave.
Eugene, OR 97405
website: www.cyberbully.org

The Center for Safe and Responsible Internet Use helps young people keep themselves safe and respect others on the Internet. Its website contains information designed to help people learn about responsible Internet behavior.

Childnet International
Studio 14, Brockley Cross Business Centre
96 Endwell Rd.
London SE4 2PD
United Kingdom
website: www.childnet.com

Childnet International's mission is to work in partnership with others around the world to help make the Internet a safe place for children. Its website features news; projects; general safety advice for parents, young people, and teachers; links; and other information.

Common Sense Media
650 Townsend St., Suite 435
San Francisco, CA 94103
website: www.commonsensemedia.org

Common Sense Media is an independent nonprofit organization that provides education, ratings, and tools to families to promote safe technology and media for children and teens. Its goal is to help kids thrive in a world of media and technology.

Get Net Wise

website: www.getnetwise.org

Get Net Wise is a website provided by Internet industry corporations and public interest organizations. Its goal is to ensure that Internet users have safe and constructive online experiences. The website contains information about online youth safety, security, and privacy.

Pew Research Center

1615 L St. NW, Suite 700
Washington, DC 20036
website: http://pewinternet.org

Through its Pew Internet & American Life Project, the center studies how Americans use the Internet and how digital technologies are shaping the world today. Its website has the results of numerous studies about privacy and the Internet.

Special Interest Group on Computer-Human Interaction (SIGCHI)

119 E. Union St., Suite A
Pasadena, CA 91103
website: www.sigchi.org

The SIGCHI is an international society for professionals, academics, and students who are interested in human-technology and human-computer interaction. A subgroup of the Association for Computing Machinery, the organization offers publications, hosts message boards, and holds conferences in the multidisciplinary field of human-computer interaction.

Stay Safe Online

website: www.staysafeonline.org

The website of the National Cyber Security Alliance offers educational materials, information for home users on protecting their computers and their children, cyber security practices, videos, a self-assessment quiz, and additional information on online safety.

ZDNet

www.zdnet.com

ZDNet provides news coverage and analysis on technology trends. Its "Mobility" section discusses how wireless carriers, machine-to-machine connections, and new devices are affecting productivity.

For Further Research

Books

Lisa J. Amstutz, *Smartphones*. Mendota Heights, MN: North Star, 2017.

Patrick Meier, *Digital Humanitarians: How Big Data Is Changing the Face of Humanitarian Response*. Boca Raton, FL: CRC, 2015.

Brian Merchant, *One Device: The Secret History of the iPhone*. New York: Little, Brown, 2017.

Carla Mooney, *How the Internet Is Changing Society*. San Diego: ReferencePoint, 2016.

Jean M. Twenge, *iGen: Why Today's Super-Connected Kids Are Growing Up Less Rebellious, More Tolerant, Less Happy—and Completely Unprepared for Adulthood*. New York: Atria, 2017.

Internet Sources

Amber Case, "Are Our Devices Turning Us into a New Kind of Human?," interview by Guy Raz, *TED Radio Hour*, NPR, September 11, 2015. www.npr.org/templates/transcript/transcript.php?storyId=438944317.

Jenny Davis, "How Do Smartphones Affect Human Thought?," *Cyborgology*, March 12, 2015. https://thesocietypages.org/cyborgology/2015/03/12/how-do-smartphones-affect-human-thought.

Carolyn Gregoire, "You Probably Use Your Smartphone Way More than You Think," *Huffington Post*, November 2, 2015. www.huffingtonpost.com/entry/smartphone-usage-estimates_us_5637687de4b063179912dc96.

Pew Research Center, "Digital Life in 2025," March 11, 2014. www.pewinternet.org/2014/03/11/digital-life-in-2025.

Elizabeth Segran, "The Case Against Smartphones," *Fast Company*, August 15, 2014. www.fastcompany.com/3034462/the-case-against-smart phones.

Jean M. Twenge, "Have Smartphones Destroyed a Generation?," *Atlantic*, September 2017. www.theatlantic.com/magazine/archive/2017/09 /has-the-smartphone-destroyed-a-generation/534198.

Tim Wu, "If a Time Traveller Saw a Smartphone," *New Yorker*, January 10, 2014. www.newyorker.com/tech/elements/if-a-time-traveller-saw-a -smartphone.

Yo Zushi, "Life with a Smartphone Is Like Having a Second Brain in Your Pocket," *New Statesman*, February 22, 2017. www.newstatesman .com/science-tech/2017/02/life-smartphone-having-second-brain-your -pocket.

Index

About the Author

Bradley Steffens is an award-winning poet, playwright, novelist, and author of more than thirty-five nonfiction books for children and young adults. He is a two-time recipient of the San Diego Book Award for Best Young Adult and Children's Nonfiction: his *Giants* won the 2005 award, and his *J.K. Rowling* claimed the 2007 prize. Steffens also received the Theodor S. Geisel Award for best book by a San Diego County author in 2007.